burntdistrict

a journal of contemporary poetry

burntdistrict

a journal of contemporary poetry

Editors
Liz Kay & Jen Lambert

Volume 3 Issue 1
Winter 2014

Omaha, NE

Table of Contents

TABLE OF CONTENTS

Table of Contents

TABLE OF CONTENTS

MAUREEN ALSOP

Crimes Tonight

Into the tell of it I asked. The grass tugged at the river. Once the blindman. Once
the mirror's foam. I followed your image: weed, trail, song. This was survival.
Itinerant face, I was warned into the falling mountain. But consider this.
Consider we could only dream doors open to finish. Meanwhile each city we
passed burned under that same old sun.

ALEXANDER LUMANS

What We Don't Know About Natalie Portman Can Still Hurt Us

Natalie Portman is a calving glacier. She is not
        long for this world before she turns
        a series of colorful, textbook evaporations.
And rumor has it
        she was once an invasive school of Asian carp,
but she kept landing facedown in our ice chests.   Twice,
                she made a living
by selling those silver collector spoons—who *doesn't*
have this empty space inside his heart? In the eye of the storm?
        Natalie Portman is No Man's Land.
And those ambient sound players—
                        the kind with settings like "Whales"
        and "Whales Talking"
and "Whales Talking about How They're Surprised
that We (Humans) Know that They (Whales) Can Talk"?
        —that's her.
And me? I was born late with the distinct desire
                to collect all things porcelain:
                1) Dolls
                2) Natalie Portman's zygomatic bone
                3) Butter dishes
Naturally, I found my way back to the sea, only to find it
        had risen. And was backward.
                                I blame her.
        O Natalie, no one knows where the afterlife starts,
only that we're always tacking in that one direction,
        chewing gum that's *just* lost its cotton candy flavor.
Come winter, you detect a lot of buzz with a lot of info
                                that's not right.
The truth about Natalie Portman is that her heart is growing
        on the outside of her body.   I believe this is it.
Too dangerous to do anything around here but stay the same.
        Having once been startled by the line
                        "the sight startled him,
like a drawer flung open to an intimacy of spoons,"
I had three hundred questions.   Namely: is "intimacy"
a hive term—as in a pod of cetaceans

or a 16-piece dinnerware set
of Aegean Mist?   Second: why am I all of a sudden
crying?   She is a glass-bottom boat.
A thousand thousand years ago
Natalie turned to ice. Watch closely as I extract a core sample.

Catherine Bresner

Dear Mucha,

It is raining in Manhattan. I am sitting in a chair overlooking 14th street and I realize you were right. I told you that people are taller than buildings. I told you that there are many green places in the city. Look at Central Park, for instance.

In the morning pink light falls across hardwood floor, spreading out like a thousand peonies, and I imagine that it is a greeting from you. But it is nighttime now, and raining so it makes no difference if I tell you a few real things. Today I saw a billboard advertising cigarettes and in a fit of frenzy went home and burned dinner.

And could you love me if I was pretty enough to be painted on your billboards? I would let my hair down long enough to collect pools of curls at my waist. I would pose naked in front of your tall landscapes and reach out with both arms pulling this city into my body.

And Mucha, the weather is all over this house.

I thought of such things while walking to a shop to buy cigarettes. In Manhattan, the streets smell like a wet cement and baked bread. It feels like the whole city is yawning. I, too, am tired of this body.

Yours,
Catherine

Catherine Bresner

Dear Mucha,

You did not tell me that you could sing. Your voice is deep and husky as if you are the type to drink whiskey while painting. When you whisper, your voice is the front door of an old house easing back into its hinges. But this means nothing if you aren't singing.

Speaking is strange and I find it harder each day to pick up the phone and say goodbye. Voices are replaced with cursors, and Paris is closer each day but I can't speak the language.

I am a like a lighthouse sending signals across the Atlantic. And each day I look for a nod. And the stars blink twice. And the phone rings for no one. And the train rolls in screaming, and the tides pull out sighing.

Love,
Catherine

Simon Perchik

You can still make out the stars
though it's noon and the beach
changes —you can tell by the feel

and listening for engine scrap
breaking apart, smelling from smoke
expects you to stand up barefoot

keep struggling with shoreline
—you're not new to this
will start the grill weeks ahead

as if stars are never sure
are milling around, forgot all about
the darkness you're breathing in

and no way now to pick and choose
the fires however small or close
to some ocean or daylight

till it creaks and your mouth
no longer lit for kisses
and songs about nothing.

Simon Perchik

The dead are already holding hands
and what's left they share
as memories —in the meantime

who do you suppose makes this tea
and the smoked fish, then room
for the grandchildren you almost forgot

were born later —the dead
are no better at it than you
—they mix up dates and places

though what pins them down
is no longer the flowers
soothed by each other and vague streams

—no, it wasn't you lifting this cup
passing itself off as empty
with nothing inside to unwrap

—from the start the dead form a circle
as if they still expect to sing out loud
and you would hear it, open your mouth.

Simon Perchik

All day and your arms
need the smock loose
and white gloves

—this barnacle is the kind
that spirals toward the light
already nurses

on a rock half at anchor
half this kitchen table
—a small loaf and already

ravenous though once it's cut
it begins to circle closer
and what your arms free

is no longer joined at the heart
born over and over
as twins facing each other

lets you see your own lips
and in the darkness
that belongs to you both.

Poet's Guide to the Jumping Frenchmen of Maine

Don't take advantage; don't stare at limbs
flailing wildly, bodies stretched like
asterisks against white snow's backdrop.
Don't shout obscenities or phrases
in obscure languages simply to see
if you'll hear them back. (You will.)
Don't demand a jumper, knife in hand,
aim it at dartboard on the room's opposite end;
he will listen, he will throw without
assessing risks: waitress walking you
another beer to keep Maine's shrill wind
from silencing your will to live. Other
plaid-fitted lumberjacks less believing
in the body's flaws, of some small amino
acid to slow these overactive responses.
Don't think the noise must be
spectacular—pistol explosion, shined ax
collapsing balsam firs—only sudden.
Unexpected window fall or car door's slam
could startle them into frenzy,
even their loved ones fair game.
Don't annoy a jumper, compel him
against his will to imitate pig-grunt
or complex hand-clap; don't make him
beg for peace as he echoes some ridiculous
shout or motion you've pitilessly directed
his way, cruel reminder of his blue-blooded
heritage, lumber camp royalty's only heirloom:
to ventriloquize your pain, your hate.

FRANCESCA BELL

Things I'd Prefer to Forget

How you placed each gun
in my hands like a live thing,
a coiled spring, a promise.

The .45 with its heft and kick.
Its full clip I learned
to slide in and then empty.

The sound when you cocked
your shotgun in the house.
It said, *Put up your hands, bitch.*

How I jumped, unable to swim,
into the cold of Bitterroot Lake
because you wanted me to waterski.

Your photographs where I don't show:
only the rope, the black lake, the spray
of something being dragged.

That you could hit *anything*—
gophers, songbirds, grouse
you brought home for dinner.

I hated to eat them.
Their tiny breast meat.
Their easy-snap bones.

Snakes you killed as a boy
with your little bow,
standing on their tails to shoot them.

Your hands clasped
around my throat
during love.

All those flowers
you sent
in apology.

Conditionals of Grief

If there is an exact equation you can apply to solve
the problem of the volunteer firefighter, his cells swelled
with off brand whiskey & how perfectly his son will recreate
the tendency to self destruct, then there is sand
between the sheets, drifting in & out of a woman who wakes
up one morning & is old.

If the men are faceless, interchangeable,
Irish & freckled & dead in other boroughs then the boys
will disappear in the same darkness & the girls they fuck
in high school will grow old & no one will ever leave.

If the water laps at the shore, tongues without teeth, murmuring
to the locals that the ground will not bear bodies, then the fathers
& sons will lie elsewhere out in Brooklyn, & the whole
wide beach will stretch out emptied & this place & its men
will remain untenable.

The First Time I Kissed Her

We were in the bathtub and it was just us
and the tub was empty and it was strange
to sit in an empty place—white as bone
and dry as bone and robbed of its purpose.

I didn't want to do it. No, I did. I wanted to
peel back her cracked lips or peel back love—
the word, what it actually is underneath
the sound and what it does to the body.

I didn't want to kiss her but I was born
to do it. I loved my little sister and our father,
watching over, smiling, and the camera
lens, smiling and there was no water

in the bathtub so I knew it wasn't bath time
and there was nothing else to do.

McKinley Murphy

More or Less

One day soon I will show up your doorstep. It's easy. It's always stooping.
Lucidly I wish to lure thoughts from streams. Sometimes you have to push
through ice if necessary and even if not, even if January. Even if it's your father
you're following down the trail, even if you wish this, too, wasn't a metaphor.
When your father rewards your joie de vive by drying your feet with his own
shirt, don't read into that, either.

Sometimes a symbol is Braille: the right language, the wrong presentation.
Sometimes are times to reflect. Some symbols are bread, too. But you need the
right knife. Or you need no knife. If I score a tree in the top of my loaf, do we
read this as more or less a symbol. (More or less). Moral-less. Molasses, too, is
seductive but only in desperation. A symbol requiring sympathy. I'd lend ears of
corn if I could spare time. I'd shuck them while you fire the grille, waiting for the
moment when it speaks. I took the light as a sign of something I knew-not-what
in the stove was going on winter nights. It's the pops I liked, the lurching forward
logs straining at the grate.

If you go away hungry, it's your own damn fault. I won't force this on you, but I'll
leave it on the table, next the bread knife.

Paula C. Lowe

Jamie Here I Am/Toe Hold/Dust

I am absent in the house
of catastrophes to come,
the house boarded up
before or after the cyclone,
the dust storm, the rise
of the tide into the second floor.

I am absent in the way that lips
leave lips, skin flaking into wind.

—Jamie asks where I've gone,
asks scrub trees and small listeners.

Say, I am in the lineup on Easter Island,
I am in the crushed stone under asphalt
on a road to the south, to the ever hopeful
but ever bleak south.

Say too, I am an afterthought
rinsed out of cheese cloth
from a time of milk and cows and grass,
a thought to cry, oh, stop sucking on the tits

of this planet, you empires who refuse to grow up:
inside bassinettes, playing with thin screen gadgets,
playing with buttons instead of toes.

—And that is it, Jamie, who can keep a reason
for toes when no one counts on them?

The man who lost everything steals
something from his neighbor.
The girl who lost her virginity,
searches for it on her knees.

—And that it is, Jamie, each village on the edge
of the earth has too few hands to keep bodies
from leaving their people.

SANDY LONGHORN

The Calendar is Turned, the Year Anointed

January, the First

Dear Madame—

They've wrapped my eyes with gauze
      forcing the lids closed
            against the fevered light.
They've swaddled my arms to my chest,
      attached more tubing & alarms.
I dictate these words in an empty room,
          where they fall
    to damp sheets & dissolve.
I know by the sound of footsteps
      and the rustle of starched cotton
when to let my lips
    flutter to a close. I separate the whitecoats
      from the nurses by each touch,
          each breath.
    One has fingers smooth as the piano keys
in the great arcade;
      one rough calloused skin that abrades.
    Their breath brings coffee,
        mints, stagnant meat.
Madame, I am hollowed & hallowing.
      They say the symptoms
    returned on the solstice. I grew aggressive
in my agitation,
      became the bird that hurls itself
against the pane, threatened by its own reflection.
    They say I drew blood,
    but I cannot find the scars.
Minus fingers, I memorize these lines and channel
      your voice,
        chanting in the dark.

—Your Immovable

11 General Orders of a Nurse

Take charge of this fevered body and its possessions.

Walk the floor in a medical manner, antiseptic & mask at the ready.

Report all violations of temperature or pulse, the staggered breathing.

Become a pure conduit of the prescription without question.

Give over the pen, the chart when the clock relieves.

Transmit all orders & incidents to whomever follows, offering the code.

Talk to no one except in the line of duty, conversation a distraction ill afforded.

Press the red intercom of alarm only on the hint of death, as in a fire raging in the blood.

Call the whitecoat listed in the book of hours for events not covered here.

Attend all whitecoats who may appear, even unscheduled, keeping eyes downcast & humble.

Be most watchful at night, a time of challenge when the body senses any lapse and the fever leaps by degree.

Jeff Tigchelaar

All That's Happened Since Kristen Spilled Beer on Our Carpet

Grandpa died. We quick made plans to pack and fly to Michigan. The luggage got lost in Milwaukee. Everyone and everything arrived, eventually. The day after getting back to Kansas, we turned around and drove to Chicago for that conference. Virginia was a no-show, and we were sad about that; we're pretty sure we know what it meant. We picked up the kids in Iowa, where they'd been stashed with your parents. Sam had blown out his pants and your dad changed a diaper for the first time in his life. "If anyone is changed, it's me," he said. Halfway through Missouri the family meltdown began. It's one thing that's never unexpected. We solved it with a ten-dollar pizza from a Casey's. We sat in the car and ate it in the dark. We didn't know gas station food could be that good. The silence was nice at first, but when it was too much I slipped in my favorite CD. You said "Now is not the time for Sinead O'Connor." I disagreed, and grabbed the last two pieces of pizza. I sulked for the next few hours. The children made us listen to Yo Gabba Gabba. Somehow we got home, and the Tigers got Prince Fielder. Whitney Houston died in her bathtub, and was only 48 years old. I had no idea she was that young. I'm in my thirties, and she was Whitney Houston already when I was around five. I'll never forget the time she guest-starred on Silver Spoons. "I think I'm in love with Whitney Houston," said Dexter, and then of course I was, too. Good Lord. Now Kristen's gone, and the stain is still here. What has it been, a month?

Home is in the Wind

I ask myself only this each greying morning:
are you pure yet? Usually the answer is:
it's a no from me. But like they all say, before I get there
there's no way I'm leaving.

Yet I'm not like those talent-show never-gos -
I don't cry, just clench my jaw
and concentrate to disappear beneath
the fine coffee-mug ring of instant, true-fold grit
that circles daily further round this life.

That means nothing much but *I'm going to try again.*
I smoke and smoke and wash my hair in ash.

[Give me the valley of an actress's beach hipbones,
the love of my grudging mother,
a white ward light I can vanish underneath.]

But the nights get more boring the less I sleep.
Under the moon it resolves itself to me:
I want to be feather-light. *I've got
a lot of hope for this.* Need to be crescent-slight.

The Rain Alone

Suddenly, love, you are
A skein of chili peppers
Making the sky equidistant
To the sky, which is such
A bright and hugely blue
Thing

    Just as the bushes
Go silver in the faltering
Blush, the sky becomes
Absolutely new in a way
That not even newness is
Wont to be but for you
Looking at it in just that
Way, which is queerly lit
With wonder and
Unexpectedness and is
The most colorful of trees

    Desert mouse
Darting between, you are
Ever only that matchless
Joy we sometimes barely
See, and are perfectly
At ease in the smallness
That you clothe yourself in
That is the smallness first
Of the pebble carved by
Rain, and then of the rain
Alone

John A. Nieves

And the Past to the Pigeons (Puer)

Later, it was only damage that strafed
the gutters in rough wind, only the haze
left when hate finds its place among old
cans and older condoms. Half a black

plastic comb wedged into a Styrofoam cup
with the remnants of what might have been
chili. Everything outlasting the touch
that defined it: footless shoes, barless

wrappers. And here, our offering. Names sprayed into
the rain course, into the muck course, cleared now by the toe
of my boot. And why should I listen to thrown stones that barely
hit the dirt hard enough to dimple a symbol, to tell me violence
was the answer, to order me, as reconciler, to scour these
letters from this concrete, to rub out, to rub? And earth
never spoke clearly in my estimation, but we listened
clearly. We obeyed. The augury—more command than

sign—tore us back to this should-be-faded memoryscape
to scrape our own names to dust. To consign monument
to the angry groaning gale, we must crush our teeth
against our teeth, must trust destruction to its work.

Persephone Writes Her Mother

He promises I will learn to burn
beneath his gaze; that if I close my eyes

and tell him where to put his hands,

I'll hear the babbling brook where I used to bathe. I'm always
thirsty. He says the body is a ladle. He says

you've set the world above us on fire
and all the rivers are flowing backwards. He says

the sky is falling, that the calves in the fields cannot drink
from their mother's teat, and the grass doesn't remember

being green. He says it's my fault,
that if only I'll soften beneath him, the sky will open.

His eyes are tongues, his arms, twine. I can't sleep,
and when I dream, it's always the same: you lean in to kiss

the top of my head, and I am pulled under. My hair, once famous to the sun,
gone anonymous,

fused with the old cottonwood's roots.

Persephone, Stumbling Into The Light

It hurts. All of it. The sun. The salted air.
Those red flowers. Their swollen tongues;

The heiffer's udder, raw
and dragging on the ground.

The men whose children were starved out
by Mother's rage bow their heads

when I pass. When they kiss
the hem of my dress, Mother calls it *reverence.*

But I know when night falls,
hardened by the newly wet earth,

these men turn towards their wives,
and grin, slide their tongues

over their teeth as they remember
my story, imagining me bound and writhing

beneath them,
a pale fish hooked and split.

Persephone Resists

I'm a sliver of light under a shut door,
a scythe, a parable whispered at bedtime,

my sex, the cure and the curse,
that cinches me into this dress fashioned

from shadows, wedding me to the moment

I was taken. Stop holding vigil.
Forget me. Let the grass green.

I don't want to be a warning,
the siren you sound

when your daughters,
under guise of picking flowers, wander

out of earshot, whispering,

He loves me. He loves me not.

On a Hill Overlooking a City

Those little flags of town
could be toothpick top
for all these grinning
know. Maybe if we'd lived
under a different sun
we'd say good luck
a little less. Flowers
might tilt like little drunks
in their borrowed clothes.
However concerned we might be
a gazelle would be
doubly, born as it is
spring-wired and bounding.
A gazelle must not know though
how inaccurately we measure
loss. How likely it is
to be at a bus stop again
combing hair in a mirror
or looking at something
very far away. How
we all keep hummingbirds
in our pockets but forgot
long ago the reason
for carrying such things.

from **We will Never be Famous**

We will be happy again.
We will gather like news
of a famous death.
We will collect star thistle
and make necklaces, yellow
necklaces. The hill
will be our rogue sovereign
state. Our children will
run like a river of bulls.
In town we will miss the ringing
of phones, not the ten-cent ditties
of cells, but the bring bring of old
ways, the clutch of eggs
in a tree I called "Doug."
Memory will not resolve itself.
In gaze or at all. I only want
an imperfect breakfast and time
to watch the digitized planet.
Fill my cup and take my body.
There are so many ways
to be perfect but who wants
to sing anymore?

Jeff Whitney

from **We will Never be Famous**

Pain used to be dangerous
but these days we have better things to do.
For instance, when was the last time
you fed snow to a geriatric horse?
Watched your teeth come in?
Waited in the night for your father?
Made a picnic just to watch the others
eating picnics? Yes we are fields:
our death is a snore and the business
of everyone. When something drags
on the carpet, we spray it. When there is a life
to end, we end it. We make like
trees, we make like sacks of bricks.
If there is some falling to do,
allow me. We burn the way
money burns, yes, we come back
wholer than before.

ARAN DONOVAN

on the up and up

gallows make order
of witches and new
colonies but to find a ladder
trained up this building like
a climbing rose—there's no
way past it even
for a simple task
like groceries.
I am so recently
recovered: my shadow kept
circumference of
me, a pack of dogs
leashed shortly and insisting
on words like marooned.
like eggs.
craters
of the moon are named
for loneliness or
Spanish governors, but I
am on the up and up,
compiling grocery lists:
no gate, no Beatrice, the moon
is not for you.

Aran Donovan

Dear,
The beggars up and down Elysian Fields adopt
beatific gestures, hold palm up to stop
the angel or lift middle and index, benediction. Even now,
I keep assuming the world means things. That the praying mantis
wasn't named for nothing, that when I can't find
a parking spot, I was not intended
to enter the building.
Yours.

MARVIN SHACKELFORD

Witchy

I keep a journal on the joys of being
your broomstick. We sweep the porch,
nonchalant but lovingly while the neighborwives
scream for their husbands from picture windows
up and down the street, and soon as dark hits
we jet for the Old World's Vegas.
I remind you: The myth comes from drugs
and how easily they slip
through a mucous membrane. Do you remember
how it used to be just dirt with us?
I'll make careful note of your answer.
Your hair tossed back moonlit and knees
pointy out in the air—sweet shit.
Rock and I'll head whatever direction you want.

JENNIFER MARTELLI

Seated Figure with Hat

We can't know if she's beautiful:
the artist painted his wife
looking away from him: the brim
of her brown fedora low over her temple,
covering the spot I test for fever
with my lips on my children, the spot
that hits the table corners always.

She is a hieroglyph: flat and all
angles: her nose under the brim,
her raised chin, a bit of black pageboy,
her breasts under her dark sleeveless shirt:
90 degrees, more or less. Maybe she is
so beautiful to him, he can't bear to paint her face or
she knows he won't eat her heart anyway
when she offers it.

She holds a glass of clear drink and
we can see through it, to her skirt,
red, and the lower steps he makes of her body:
her arm crooked on the chair, resting on its arm,
her lap, and all the blacks, the blood red, and you know
it's fall because of the layers of golden
yellow that fill the rest of the canvas. Each angle,

each V he painted, catches the overflow of color: gold
like whiskey into and out from her, like the day something dies,
late in the fall's afternoon. One of them wanted a god,
one of them wanted to be a god.
In the end, nothing is ever healed by this.

The title is also the title of the painting "Seated Figure with Hat" -
Richard Diebenkorn, 1967

Hosta Bed

Foolish stones, they push up
toward his yard like wings
taking the black wind under them.
To dig a garden is to have
a flock of ruddy finches explode
out of the earth.

All those years leaning toward
Parousia, he never knew
these great bodies of lime and chert
in their own resurrection, the slow
hail of rock and wreck
before our own sailing.

Wolf visits her dream

years after the nasty
episode, Grandmother gone now,
the forest suffering from blight.

He would have her drink the long
glass of wine from crystal where the three
small bones of the ear lay listening.

Why couldn't she move to another
story. Why did he do the Russian dance
until she promised to kiss.

There's no mercy in the eight-bedroom
house he's built next to the pond. In Timberwood
Acres, pigs are rolling out the sod.

What eyes he had, even as
she refused them. What teeth, what crooked fences
along the straight streets of dream.

She wants to move, awake, to another
story, the one where she drifts large as a red front
across the continent, sea to sea.

She wants to move to the story of red
rain falling on the blight, making the brown
trees green, the brown birds sing.

The title is a first line by Suheir Hammad, from "break (full)."

Katrina Conjures Gumbo
Bayou's kitchen, September 2005

Simmer in a kitchen where the crook of a wooden spoon
often begs for mercy on the burn of an eye; a whole

stick & a half of butter & a teaspoon of flour
blanket the bottom of a skillet the way

naked soles seethe on a rooftop, ripen jaundice
& rhythms in flicks of backlash like mudbugs.

Today's menu: FEMA flew over Marie Lauveau's
X-marked grave. The aerial view over the deep

bowl of surrender-white tee flags of rice grains
graffiti with black spray paint campaigns, pungent

with rescues & "fuck yous!" let off steam in casual
Creole: a seafood melody, filé & onions, & a roux

of missing persons & isolated identities solicit
like bodies of crawfish sopped in okra & tomatoes

after the president's flipped French Quarter spun,
tales like Chef Leah Chase's etouffé recipe swaps

before burials in seasoned, soot-rousse. Say grace
for the nourishment of our bodies, for Christ's sake.

KATHARINE DIEHL

Little Peach Song

And druzy and drupe fruits
like peaches I boil
                and place in a cold bowl
so the skin slips off whole, give me comfort
                when houseplant leaves turn
and go black and pale-
                belly fish beg to be fed
specks of egg
                yolk are left
on my knife on the table
                with the dark finish, oh my
pink shirt has a knot
                in it, last night
I dropped you in your bath
                on your head, I can't
say more about it

GRACE GARDINER

Barefoot in Virginia Blue Ridge

You tell me to put on my shoes.
I dally with the straps, sneak
my webbed toes across the rocks
into the lull of the river once more.
Normally I can't wait to get the hell
out of moments like this one, but it's you
who's slapping green water
from your knees, coughing briskly
as you thrust on your boots.

> [I know now it was she you were so eager
> to get to, though a couple of years away then,
> she kept waiting to kiss the ends of your hair
> like I had wanted you to kiss mine.
> That day the river felt young, as did I,
> and your eyes, though heavy under their lids,
> were still in the early stages of breaking.]

My hand slips inside your palm,
the calluses rougher than I remember.
It could just be the woods and the deer
you skinned earlier, the jaw bone hard
in your hands and you lifting pink ribbons
of flesh as if stripping a daisy of its petals.

> [Your own version, I'm sure, of I-love-you,
> I-love-you-not, circling in your head
> as the deer withered, warm in your hands.
> *This stringy cheek means I love her.*
> *This slab of shoulder means*—I know.]

I'm not sure where we're going, but up ahead
I hear crows and the horses whinnying.
I wish we could see the cows again, the calves
suckling on their mothers and rolling in the river.

We were just laughing together like them,
mouths bellowing and noses nudged close.

　　　[How blurred it has become,
　　　as if I've swallowed you halfway,
　　　as if I've picked you from my teeth,
　　　washed the scab off my knees.
　　　Yet there remains the scar's flicker;
　　　still here, the throbbing of gums;
　　　even now, the everlasting heave.]

A gunshot: I shrink into you,
then come the crows—five, seven, thirteen
erupt from their perches, puncturing
the sky, dark and dry as leaves.

　　　[And in the silence after
　　　you, my grandmother's voice ringing:
　　　Sing a song of sixpence,
　　　A pocket full of rye.
　　　Four and twenty blackbirds,
　　　Baked in a pie.]

Your hands lie tense on my waist,
the recoiling so faint, I'm not sure it's there.
So I tug you close, squeeze your sides
to spark the green in your eyes.

　　　[You winced *when the pie was opened,*
　　　the birds began to screech.
　　　And me, *eating bread and honey,*
　　　no, *hanging out the clothes,* no,
　　　when down came a blackbird
　　　and pecked off—you know.]

I get a twinge of your lips, a sigh I take
as tired, the end of a kiss on my forehead.
We walk back to camp, close enough
to smell the same, though our hands
are empty now, dried of the river.

BARBARA DUFFEY

So when tomorrow folds
in on itself like an ache
I'll visit your voice in the
nest of my want, your shelter.
Baby—please need me shorn
and scalded, needled. I shut myself
down to let science take over your
outset, my makeshift tiny specimen.

Draw What Is There

In art class, the instructor says
Draw your hand—not an

idea of hand but what is really there.
My pencil scratches over paper,

telling truth. Wrinkles.
Crookedness and bulges.

I let the ring fall to the side,
as it often does, let the tunneling

veins go where they have to go,
but left out is this:

the day I pulled your hair,
my son,

when you broke something.
It was too much, all of it.

Not the green plastic
forgettable trifle you broke;

I mean my work, my union with your father.
It was too much and it was too little

and there you were, young and perfect
and close by my hand. You say

you don't remember
so I don't mention it again

but I remember and
have not let it go.

Let me turn my hand over, watch
the ends of the fingers catch light,

notice that knuckles are only creases
over the bones that do the work.

Let me see what is
in front of me, opening and closing.

Let what I did and failed to do
drop like a leaf from my hand.

Cabo de Sao Vicente

On a stone scrambling
down the coast
from Sagres
we descended
like steps. You
led- your broad
back, my anchor
point. She followed,

a pink wooden fish
on a stick in one
hand, my hand
in the other. I
was last, bracing
her to the cliff wall
when the breeze
picked up. Rusty

poles jammed
into the stone, curled
at the top where a rope
once fed through, were
all we had
to grip. To

our right
the cliff face. To
the left
the air, just
a misstep
from the churning
sea, bashing
itself against a fissure
where once North America
locked into this crumbling
red earth. We stopped

MAGGIE SMITH HURT

at the bottom, shocked
at the closeness
of the desperate
sea. I stood
back from you. We
had come all this way,
to the westernmost
point of Europe
to discuss how
we would leave
one another. But

instead, we
scrambled down this
dangerous and broken

trail, protecting
the one between us
from the dense,
cold desolation of
the sea. This blue
and startling vastness.

LAUREN GORDON

My Daughter Crying In Morning Light on a Thursday

This day is not entitled to this rich sun,
bright jacket of content.

Shadow and light splay across her body:

a piano wire, a brass horse, a yellow bouquet
blossoming against her stomach, bridal—

then full sunshine conquers the shell of November's atmosphere
and swims intimately on the sill;

a breaststroke that blasts the family room into an ease
of buttery plaids and warmth

until there is no departure

from the race to add joy, to illuminate a moment, be present
each goddamned golden second.

Lauren Gordon

This Horror Will Grow Mild, This Darkness Light

My love poem is a strange dog, Joel says I have lived close
between walls, those kinds of weeks
where the baby grows fast and eats

like I invented the kitchen

this turned out with some good.

Once it was a betrayal I had to leave before
my first husband could get a doctorate in something other than I'm sorry

why did I have many many many loves?

I had just taken tears into my arms
when I thought crazy, I was doing my life
as I liked, my threatening sense of righteousness
wrong. Then

it took years, stuck them to its throat
spit them out until every seed looked stupid
and nothing felt like anything or it felt like a hotel key card
or one of those pens that writes upside down—

Contingency looked like this: Joel

says I feel silver when I wake up, that the baby
has given me a local career in coffee, that there is talk
of small life with parts green and sappy, a fresh stem

we cut and spliced to a dry stick.

They Are Farmers

My family farmed honey. By name
we whispered to our hired hands:
mud dauber, doppelganger.

Honey wadded chlorophyll
deep in its golden handkerchief,
and honeybees traced the leaves

back to their births—fused
vertebrae dotting a branch.

Pollen rose hives around my neck.

The honeysuckle and its subtle
breath burnt like cane in autumn

when I inhaled. Kerosene,
lightning strike. That autumn,
I buried so much honeysuckle

with ashes in the flue of our field.
The twitching legs of honeybees
mechanistic within the flames.

Brian Clifton

Translucent

In verse, the bees' sleek repetitions glitter
the screen. Their legs jitter as metal switches
galvanizing in electric sync.

In reverse, the VCR flutter-folds honeycombs
and honey bears. It satisfies my want of a screw
stripping the flecks of nickel-plate.

Fast-forward to the branches' unfeathering,
the bees' twitch 'n time, and how such flitting
spins the pollen's glitter into goo.

Slow their twirling hum from white noise
to bass thrum, then pull back. Watch their hives
suck them in again. A clean horizon.

But the World's First Bioluminesent Rabbit Hasn't Left the Lab

It must be hard
to always wake
to the same kind
of morning. The one
that seems to say
there's never been
a sun to save.
The one that strokes
you with shadows
and taunts you
with Eduardo's
ghostly hush:
Me beijar.
Me beijar, minha filha.
Never mind
the poppy field dreams;
every morning
is a broken promise
confettied
with the trappings
of rabbitdom. A fresh
mineral lick morning
is never enough
to forget you're
forgotten and unfree.

Megan Hudgins

The World's First Bioluminescent Rabbit and the Insta-Aunt

My brother will soon marry a woman with two children.
I dreamt of Eduardo before they arrived. Mi sobrino,

flushed and in love with his new family, holding me
tight around the waist. But Eduardo is ten and the king

of everything. Monopoly and darts and Uno Stacko
and being bilingual. And drawing whatever you like.

My brother insists, Tía Megan. Ella es tu tía. Eduardo
will not call me his aunt, but he asks what I would like

him to draw. For my birthday present. And when
is my birthday? He can send it to me. He can draw anything.

I ask about a rabbit, and can it be green? We are gringos
speaking Spanglish to him and his little sister, feeding

them white and brown casseroles of German origin.
He is bored here, in the fields of rural Illinois, and he will not

call me tía, but, if that's what I want, a green rabbit
is what I will get. His sister is skeptical, too, of this insta-aunt,

but after we play with Sponge Bob, we are old friends,
sharing a pillow and blanket on the couch. Mi sobrina.

For Christmas, my mother had sent Eduardo a mini
microscope set. He is king of the microscope, king

of science class. Bow to me, hermanita! he says,
but she shows him her tongue. He sighs. Someday,

you will all bow to me. And months after they've gone,
a drawing arrives in the mail. The rabbit is kelly green,

her lines traced from an Easter card or coloring book.
I stare at this effigy of Alba, both of our wasteland bodies

coping with the kits of others. Insta-aunts only. Alba
dreams of Eduardo as I dream of Eduardo. We wonder
how much longer we can call him inocente.

Sally Houtman

Pivot clockwise, watch your footing on its fragile crust

because you live on this broken island,
Gondwanaland's forgotten pedestal of bone

because there is no line of demarcation
between the east and impossibility

because there is no reasoning with the tide
or greed or ghosts or gravity

because the foolish sun is halved twice a day
and the sky remains indifferent, wind-rubbed and bare

because this is no way to live, weeping over onions,
in a winter kitchen, wounds still raw, because

all the earth is just a grave that hoards
its granite, and there is no room in its sarcophagus

for silent, rusted things, because beliefs
will not rest on sturdy hinges and a memoir cannot be written

in the sand, because wishes cannot bruise the air and a swallow cannot roost
higher than it flies, because the tree does not cling to its leaves

and fruit will ripen off the vine, because a hole requires an edge to exist
and because this edge might, at any moment, fall away –

Marcus Myers

from **The Fiction We Make Between Us**

1.

The brownstone spiraled a nautilus up to me
when she returned from her shift at the wine bar.
On the bed, I listened for her through the century
of wallpaper, plaster and brick. Through the books

and movies pasted to the walls of my skull.
Beneath windows, the scrape of grit under shoes.
Most often a pair of soles dragged the quiet
of her street behind each step, but sometimes

a couple passed whose voices scuffed and tapped
their syllables along at ground-level like children
with sticks. This filled the horizon in my head
with an expanse not unlike a teenager

with a pipe before an ocean laden with stars. The stars
unbraiding from smoke he calls hope. And I wanted her
to walk through her door each time my boyhood welled up
from my torso. And I filled the passing sounds

with a bucketful of thoughts for her whenever
a couple of voices passed below. Very
similar things happened once or twice an hour,
when the brassy door pierced the foyer,

and up stood the hairs on my neck. And so I hoisted
such a workaday heft four stories, like a baby grand,
to the hungry, small bones in my ears. Her cats,
who wanted just as much to nuzzle her legs, knew

when the stairs held her exquisite shape.
When she returned, she wore the night
pinned in her hair. Until she let it fall on my chest,
where it curtained our faces from the streetlight.

Marcus Myers

2.

Mostly I lay within her lamps
those nights, waiting with anecdotes
for how I followed the hours
along South Street. The Laundromat

where I watched the all-night scent
of her debride from my sentiment, and spin
out through the gray water in the porthole.
The point of view a sinking ship affords,

if only I'd listened. The record store I entered
where the kids with patched sweatshirts
and smelly jeans slapped the jewel cases
with a dangerous grade of lust. The dusk

light un-tucked from shadow beneath the roofline,
as I walked out, admiring her city's stretches
of row house, with their facades done like heartbreaks
of China and bottle glass. The mash-up her city made

of onion, cheesesteak and beer. The bus exhaust,
the whiskey breath, the shoulder bump
the guy in leather gave me, the mirror the cherry
blossoms made of the sidewalk, the metal rub

from the historical markers beneath my fingers,
the cobblestones along my insteps
tamped down two centuries ago. I epoxied a mosaic
of my own below her rooftops to tell her.

But mostly I listened with the cats
to the foyer's hollow axis.

3.

Those few nights I did not wait up for her
shift to end, I sat at a corner table
with a face for the intersection, I hoped,
like a man who parses his thoughts

while bumping his fingers along the rosary
of headlights and taillights. But really,
I was the guy taking in her face and hands
as they passed over the mahogany room.

She was beautiful yet she could have been, I know
now, anyone else who walked home to me. Sure,
in each hand a blossom of glasses. Sure,
below her slender wrist, the wine key's pirouette.

Sure, I loved her lower lip, how she checked it
beneath her teeth as she balanced a tray.

4.

Waiting for her to return to her apartment,
I watched braids of smoke rise from the fingers
of my right hand, a wish she might ascend
the stairs. As if we could will her to pass

through those doors, I said once, and the smoke
exhausted itself against her ceiling
of phosphorous stars. The cats clenched
their eyes with their noses.

Something in their expression mirrors
something in my limbic system. What is it
about spirals, the ones in her brownstone
as they held against the bones in my skull?

What is it about these gyres I float
while daydreaming about the moment,
the commotion of those moments,
she walked through her door?

JIM PETERSON

Lust at the Lecture on Modernist Painters

1   Arrival

Body as cloud
drifting through trees,
cloud as body
morphing in the high winds.

I arrive late
and the people I know
lock elbow to elbow
within their rows.
I find a seat
next to a student,
naked feet and toe rings,
fingernails and toenails glowing blue.
Now how am I
supposed to hear the scholars
explore the transformations
of four modernists turned expressionists
sitting next to those jubilant toes?

On the screen
a long skinny hairy bodiless arm
reaches from some exterior dimension
into the still life landscape
of a room—a chair, a table, a cup
of coffee with a tuft of steam—
a unified sense of presence
and absence.

2   The Lecture

the garland of bones
the gnarled feet of gnomes

JIM PETERSON

the vegetable demon
chameleons in the corn
the foil of gusts
the sheen of morning water
chiaroscuro of a room
drama of the object frankly stellar
the vehicle of a dream
the bifurcation of smoke rings
instances of disconnection
instances of interface
the broken stroke
riding a wild image
the threshold of a drama
the modifications of motif
half organic half metallic
beyond the interplay of surface
a dissatisfaction with the containing edge
a thing in a place
a place containing things
drunken brush drunken line
drunken rain on the window
bring the hand back in
let it languish on the table
the face that is not a face
foot floating above a mattress
mouth spitting out a gold ring
the twisted torso
among the twisted sheets
evidence of desire
content is a slippery glimpse
an admiration of naked kneecaps
evidence of the incomplete motive
toe-rings on slender toes
a notion of where things fit
the out of phase phase

the biases of the eye
the call of the unknown within the known

3   Interlude

The evidence of a body
is a door
creaking open on its hinges
as if by wind,
is the hollowness
of the hallway in moonlight
or in sunlight on gray rainy days,
is the loveliness of knees
pressed together beside me—
the heaviness of walls.

4   Serious Daydream

All of us, each of us, unaware
of the genetic possibility, the potential
in the biological scheme that we are—
Lopez unaware, on the Antarctic tundra,
the last great glacier's blue receding
into white beneath his eyes—

not the blue of toenails
redefining blue for all time—

Williams unaware, among the burrowing owls,
the whimbrells, disappearing
from the marsh—

I, unaware of the great earth spinning

down my spine, a vortex of energy
pouring into my bones—feeling only
the long bone of a thigh
against the long bone of my own.

Constellations of the city
spiral in the curved distance,
consuming darkness but only for a time,
everything only for a time, darkness
a given that cannot be finally consumed—

unless it's the darkness of eyes,
then the flash of blue lids closing,
then the embodied darkness lying down again.

Imagine a mutation in the DNA
that transcends predator/prey
economics, sexual gratification
consumerism—

the blue of painted toes,
the rose of lips...

5   Afterwards

She nibbled on cheese and crackers,
the luminous blue of her nails
shimmering against the red wine.

Then she disappeared,
the cloud of a body
making its long journey
into the bodies of clouds.

JIM PETERSON

Later, I lay down in a meadow
surrounded by woods, and allowed
the shadows among the leaves of oak and birch
to grow together in full darkness around me.
The night voices rose up in scattered song.
I have seen enough of this world
to know what I love—paintings
that show me how to see
what I haven't seen: a young woman
I don't know with rings on her toes;
the earth bearing me
through space, spinning
on its own center and circling the sun,
manifesting me as this flesh among the ferns.

MICHAEL MCLANE

Settlement

The problem with trees is obscurity. You cannot see the future lumbering through the night towards you until it is already on the roof. So we cut them down and distribute them evenly among us so there can be no blame. And we are many and cold, and the trees are legion. One among us has learned to play music on a saw. Low and trembling.

CONTRIBUTORS

Maureen Alsop, Ph.D. is the author of *Mantic, Apparition Wren,* and *Mirror Inside Coffin* (forthcoming). Her poems have appeared in numerous magazines including *Kenyon Review, Tampa Review, Typo,* and *Barrow Street.* She edits poetry for *Poemeleon,* and teaches locally through the Inlandia Institute and online with the Rooster Moans poetry cooperative. www.maureenalsop.com

Francesca Bell's poems have appeared in many journals, including *Rattle, burntdistrict, North American Review, Passages North, Poetry Northwest,* and *The Sun.* New work is forthcoming in *Prairie Schooner, Crab Creek Review, Flycatcher, River Styx,* and *Tar River Poetry.* She has been nominated six times for the Pushcart Prize. Her manuscript was a finalist in the Poetry Foundation's 2012 Emily Dickinson First Book Award competition, a semi-finalist for the 2012 and 2013 Philip Levine Poetry Prize, a finalist for the May Swenson Poetry Award, and a finalist in the Carnegie Mellon 2013 open submission period. Also to her credit are three luminous and eccentric children.

Catherine Bresner is the author of the chapbook *The Merriam Webster Series.* She was the editorial assistant of Pilot Books, an intern for *The Massachusetts Review,* a participant of the Juniper Summer Writing Institute. Her poetry has been published in *The Pinch* and is forthcoming in *H_NGM_N Journal* and *The Cream City Review* . She is currently pursuing an MFA in poetry at The University of Washington, Seattle, and is the assistant editor for *The Seattle Review.*

Brian Clifton is the co-editor of *Bear Review.* His poems can be found in *Meat for Tea, Juked, PANK!,* and other magazines.

Katharine Diehl lives in Brooklyn and has been published in journals including *Squalorly, Fickle Muses,* and *Penduline.* In 2012 she attended the New York State Summer Writers Institute on scholarship; she was a 2013 finalist for the Norman Mailer college poetry contest. She blogs about the creative process and other things at frozenseawriting.tumblr.com.

Aran Donovan lives in the charming squalor of New Orleans. Once, she wanted to be a paleontologist. Her poetry has appeared in the journals *Rhino, New Ohio Review,* and *Southern Poetry Review,* and in *Best New Poets 2013.*

Contributors

Barbara Duffey is an assistant professor of English at Dakota Wesleyan University, where she teaches creative writing, composition, and literature courses. Her poetry chapbooks *The Circus of Forgetting* (dancing girl press) and *The Verge of Thirst* (South Dakota State Poetry Society) were published in 2013, and she has a full-length collection forthcoming from Word Poetry in 2015. Her poems have appeared in *Prairie Schooner, Best New Poets 2009, Western Humanities Review,* and elsewhere. She lives in Mitchell, SD, with her husband and son.

Yolanda J. Franklin's work is forthcoming or has appeared in *African American Review, Kweli, PMS:poemmemoirstory, Sugar House Review, Crab Orchard Review's American South Issue, The Hoot & Howl of the Owl Anthology of Hurston Wright Writers' Week,* and *SPECS: Journal of Arts & Culture's Kaleidoscopic Points Issue.* Her awards include a 2012 and 2014 Cave Canem fellowship, the 2013 Kingsbury Award, and several scholarships, including a summer at the Fine Arts Work Center in Provincetown, Indiana Writer's Week, and Colrain Poetry Manuscript Workshop. Her collection of poems, *Ruined Nylons,* was a finalist for the 2013 Crab Orchard Series in Poetry Award. She is a graduate of Lesley University's MFA Writing Program and is a doctoral candidate at Florida State University.

Grace Gardiner is currently earning a BFA in English with an emphasis in Creative Writing from Randolph College, where she serves as co-editor of both the literary magazine and the newspaper. In her copious amounts of free time, she roams her campus' green-space, waiting for the cherry blossoms to return.

Lauren Gordon is the author of *Meaningful Fingers* (Finishing Line Press, 2014) and *Keen* (horse less press, 2014). She is a Pushcart Prize nominated poet and her work has appeared in or is forthcoming with *Sugar House Review, [PANK], Rain Taxi, Web Del Sol, Poetry Crush, Menacing Hedge* and *Mikrokosmos/mojo.* She is a Contributing Editor to *Radius Lit* and lives outside of Milwaukee.

Sally Houtman is an ex-pat American who relocated to New Zealand in 2005. She is the author of a non-fiction book, branching into fiction and poetry in 2007. Since that time, her work has appeared in more than thirty print and online publications, earned four New Zealand writing awards, and been nominated for a 2012 Pushcart Prize.

Contributors

Megan Hudgins is a former graduate student and instructor at Southern Illinois University - Edwardsville. There, she was also the editing assistant for *Sou'Wester Literary Magazine*. You can find some of her work in *SIUE's in-house journal*, the *River Bluff Review* and online journals *Anti-* and *Toad: The Journal*. She was also featured as one of the *River Styx's* "Hungry Young Poets" just a few years ago.

Maggie Smith Hurt was born and raised in Iowa. In 1993 she moved to New York City where she received her MFA at Hunter College. She moved to Ireland in 2003 where she was a founding partner and creative writing teacher at Big Smoke Writing Factory in Dublin. In early 2012 she moved back to the Midwest and is now living in Omaha, Nebraska with her daughter Lyla. Maggie has had poems published recently in various publications in the UK and Ireland such as *Prole, Iota,* and *The SHOp*.

Michael Levan's poems have appeared recently in *Indiana Review, Mid-American Review, American Literary Review, Lunch Ticket, Tampa Review Online,* and *Heron Tree* as well as *CutBank's* 40th anniversary anthology and *Southern Poetry Anthology VI: Tennessee*. He teaches writing at the University of Saint Francis and lives in Fort Wayne, Indiana, with his wife, Molly, and son, Atticus.

Emma Lister is an A-level student who lives in the middle of a valley in deep-country Devon. She is a winner of Foyle Young Poets 2013 and the National Trust's first under-sixteens poetry competition in 2011. Other work is forthcoming in *The Blue Pencil Online*.

Sandy Longhorn is the author of *The Girlhood Book of Prairie Myths*, winner of the 2013 Jacar Press Full-Length Poetry Book Contest, and *Blood Almanac*, winner of the Anhinga Prize for Poetry. New poems have appeared in *Crazyhorse, Hayden's Ferry Review, Hotel Amerika, The Southeast Review,* and elsewhere. Longhorn teaches at Pulaski Technical College, where she directs the Big Rock Reading Series, and for the online MFA Program at the University of Arkansas Monticello. In addition, she co-edits the online journal *Heron Tree* and blogs at Myself the only Kangaroo among the Beauty.

Contributors

Paula C. Lowe lives south of town three hours north of Los Angeles. Lowe's latest book is *Moo* (Big Yes Press, 2014). Her poems appear in *Poet Lore, The Comstock Review, Tule Review, The Iowa Review, Askew, Dogwood, Sow's Ear,* and in the anthologies *Bird as Black as the Sun and Poems For Endangered Places.* She holds a graduate degree from the University of Washington and has authored a half dozen nonfiction books.

Alexander Lumans is currently the Spring 2014 Philip Roth Resident at Bucknell University. His writing has been published in *Gulf Coast, Guernica, Blackbird, Cincinnati Review, Sycamore Review, The Normal School,* among others. He has been awarded fellowships to the MacDowell Colony, Blue Mountain Center, ART342, Norton Island, RopeWalk Writers Retreat, Bread Loaf Writers' Conference, and Sewanee Writers' Conference. He is co-editor of the anthology *Apocalypse Now: Poems and Prose from the End of Days* (Upper Rubber Boot Books). He graduated from the M.F.A. Fiction Program at Southern Illinois University Carbondale

Jennifer Martelli was born and raised in Massachusetts, and graduated from Boston University and The Warren Wilson M.F.A. Program for Writers. She's taught high school English as well as women's literature at Emerson College in Boston. Her work has appeared, or will appear, in the following publications: *The Denver Quarterly, Folio, Calliope, Kalliope, The Mississippi Review, The Bellingham Review, Kindred, Bitterzoet, ZigZag Folio, The Inflectionist Review, Sugared Water, Slippery Elm, Tar River Review* and *Bop Dead City.* She was a finalist for the Sue Elkind Poetry Prize and a recipient of the Massachusetts Cultural Council Grant in Poetry. Her chapbook, *Apostrophe,* was published in 2011 by BigTable Publishing Company.

Winner of the 2011 Nebraska Book Award for Poetry for her debut collection, *Cradling Monsoons,* **Sarah McKinstry-Brown** studied poetry at The University of Nebraska and has been published everywhere from West Virginia's standardized tests to literary journals such as *South Dakota Review.* She currently teaches Creative Writing at the University of Nebraska at Omaha, and when she's not reading or teaching, you can find Sarah in Omaha with her husband, the poet Matt Mason, and their two beautiful, feisty daughters. For more info, go to: sarah.midverse.com

CONTRIBUTORS

Michael McLane lives in Salt Lake City, Utah where he works for the Utah Humanities Council. He holds an MFA from Colorado State University and is finishing a Masters in Environmental Humanities at the University of Utah. His work has appeared or is forthcoming in *Colorado Review, Laurel Review, Sidebrow*, and *Denver Quarterly*, among others. He is the review editor for *Sugar House Review* and a co-editor for the new journal *saltfront.*

Marcus Myers lives in Kansas City, MO, where he teaches social studies to gifted & talented students and raises a sassy four-year-old named Audrey. His writing has appeared in *H_NGM_N, Mid-American Review, National Poetry Review, Pleiades, Tar River Poetry, The Rumpus* and elsewhere. He and Brian Clifton co-edit *Bear Review*, the new online journal of poetry, flash fiction, and micro essays.

McKinley Murphy grew up in a log cabin in the woods of southern Missouri. She earned her B.A. at Knox College and will earn her M.A. in English at Truman State University in May 2014. In between, she worked as a grocery store checker and wrote poems on receipt paper in purple ink.

John A. Nieves has poems forthcoming or recently published in journals such as: *Beloit Poetry Journal, Southeast Review*, and *Southern Review*. He won the 2011 Indiana Review Poetry and his first book, *Curio* (2014), won the Elixir Press Annual Poetry Award Judge's Prize. He is an Assistant Professor of English at Salisbury University. He received his M.A. from University of South Florida and his Ph.D. from the University of Missouri.

Simon Perchik is an attorney whose poems have appeared in *Partisan Review, The Nation, Poetry, The New Yorker,* and elsewhere. His most recent collection is *Almost Rain*, published by River Otter Press (2013). For more information, including free e-books, his essay titled "Magic, Illusion and Other Realities" please visit his website at www.simonperchik.com.

Jim Peterson has published four full-length collections of poetry—*The Man Who Grew Silent, An Afternoon With K, The Owning Stone*, and *The Bob and Weave*— and a novel, *Paper Crown*. His poems have appeared in such journals as *Poetry, Georgia Review, Shenandoah, Poetry Northwest, Prairie Schooner, Cave Wall, South Dakota Review* etc., and have won the Benjamin Saltman Award from

Red Hen Press and a Fellowship in Poetry from the Virginia Arts Commission. He is on the faculty of the University of Nebraska MFA Program in Creative Writing, and he has recently retired as Coordinator of Creative Writing/Writer in Residence at Randolph College in Lynchburg, Virginia where he lives with his wife Harriet and their charismatic Welsh Corgi, Mama Kilya.

Derek Pollard is co-author with Derek Henderson of the book *Inconsequentia* (BlazeVOX). His poems, creative non-fiction, and reviews appear in *American Book Review, Colorado Review, Court Green, Diagram III, H_ngm_n, Pleiades,* and *Six-Word Memoirs on Love & Heartbreak,* among numerous other anthologies and journals. He is Assistant Editor at Barrow Street Press, Poetry and Nonfiction Editor at *Witness Magazine,* Managing Editor at *Interim Magazine,* and is currently a Black Mountain Institute Fellow at the University of Nevada, Las Vegas. More information can be found at www.twodereks.com.

Amber Rambharose runs Forthcoming Poets and is an Assistant Editor at YesYes Books. Her work appears or is forthcoming in *Thrush Poetry Journal, Arcadia, Muzzle Magazine,* and *Whiskey Island,* among others.

Richard Robbins grew up in Southern California and Montana. He studied with Richard Hugo and Madeline DeFrees at the University of Montana, where he earned his MFA. He has published five books of poems, most recently *Radioactive City* (Bellday Books, 2009) and *Other Americas* (Blueroad Press, 2010). He has received awards from The Loft, the Minnesota State Arts Board, the National Endowment for the Arts, and the Poetry Society of America. He directs the creative writing program and Good Thunder Reading Series at Minnesota State University, Mankato. For more about his work, see http:// english2.mnsu.edu/robbins/

Marjorie Saiser's novel in poems is *LOSING THE RING IN THE RIVER* (University of New Mexico Press, 2013). Saiser has received several Nebraska Book Awards, the Vreelands Award, and the Leo Love Award. Her work is found on the *Writers' Almanac* and in *Nimrod, Chattahoochee Review, Rattle,* and at poetmarge.com.

Contributors

Marvin Shackelford lives in the Texas Panhandle with his wife, Shea, and earns a living in agriculture. His work appears in such journals as *Confrontation, Cimarron Review, Parcel, Beloit Fiction Journal,* and *Armchair/Shotgun.* Aimless tweets @WorderFarmer.

Jeff Tigchelaar's poems appear or are forthcoming in or on *Pleiades, LIT, The Laurel Review, Court Green, Fugue, CutBank, Juked, The Offending Adam, Handsome,* and *Gertrude.*

Jeff Whitney is a co-founding editor of *Peel Press,* a new home for genre-bending literary book art. Recent poems have appeared in *Devil's Lake, Salt Hill, Thrush,* and *Verse Daily.* He lives in South Korea.

The Royal Nonesuch

Steven D. Schroeder

SparkWheelPress

GHOST AS

C DYLAN BASSETT

SparkWheelPress

SUGAR HOUSE REVIEW

AN INDEPENDENT POETRY MAGAZINE

RECENT CONTRIBUTORS

Dan Beachy-Quick	William Kloefkorn	Donald Revell
Anne Caston	Jeffrey McDaniel	Natasha Sajé
Teresa Cader	Campbell McGrath	Janet Sylvester
Major Jackson	Paul Muldoon	Pimone Triplett
Claudia Keelan	Greg Pape	Joshua Marie Wilkinson

**Work from our pages has been included in *Verse Daily, Poetry Daily*
and *2011 Pushcart Prize XXXV: Best of the Small Presses*.**

SUBSCRIPTIONS

One Year: $12   Single Issue: $7   PDF Version: $2

SUBMIT, SUBSCRIBE, PASS SUGAR HOUSE REVIEW ALONG.

P.O. Box 17091, Salt Lake City, UT 84117

www.SugarHouseReview.com

MANTIC

by

Maureen Alsop

Augury Books
ISBN: 978-0-9887355-1-4
72 pages; paperback; $12.00

"Alsop is an alchemist, possessing the uncanny gift of rendering the concrete abstract, the opaque transparent." —Lissa Kiernan, **Arsenic Lobster**

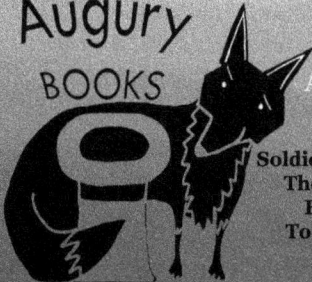

URB
UPPER RUBBER BOOT

Λρφcalypse NΟW

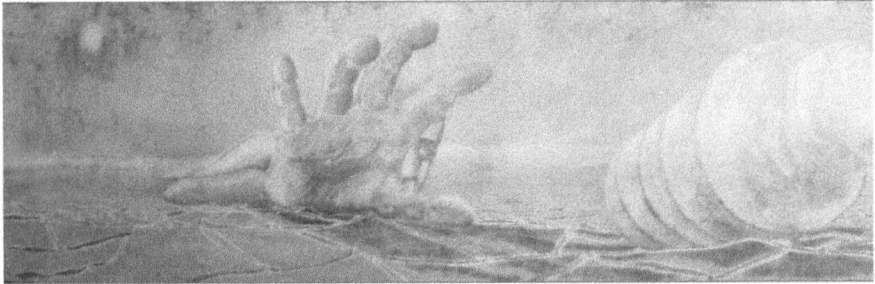

Poems and Prose from the End of Days

Edited by Andrew McFadyen-Ketchum and Alexander Lumans

Margaret Atwood, Paolo Bacigalupi, Brian Barker, Jenna Bazzell, Nicky Beer, Pinckney Benedict, Kristin Bock, Tina Connolly, David J. Daniels, Darcie Dennigan, Brian Evenson, Seth Fried, TR Hummer, Rodney Jones, Judy Jordan, Kelly Link, Alexander Lumans, Charles Martin, Davis McCombs, Andrew McFadyen-Ketchum, Marc McKee, Tessa Mellas, Wayne Miller, Simone Muench, Keith Montesano, Joyce Carol Oates, Ed Pavlić, Catherine Pierce, Kevin Prufer, Joshua Robbins, David Roderick, Jeffrey Schultz, Maggie Smith, Chet Weise, Josh Woods, E. Lily Yu.

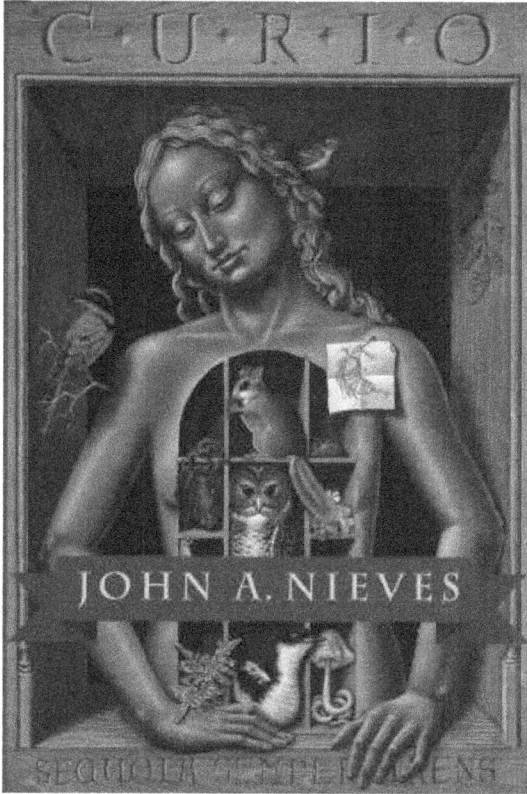

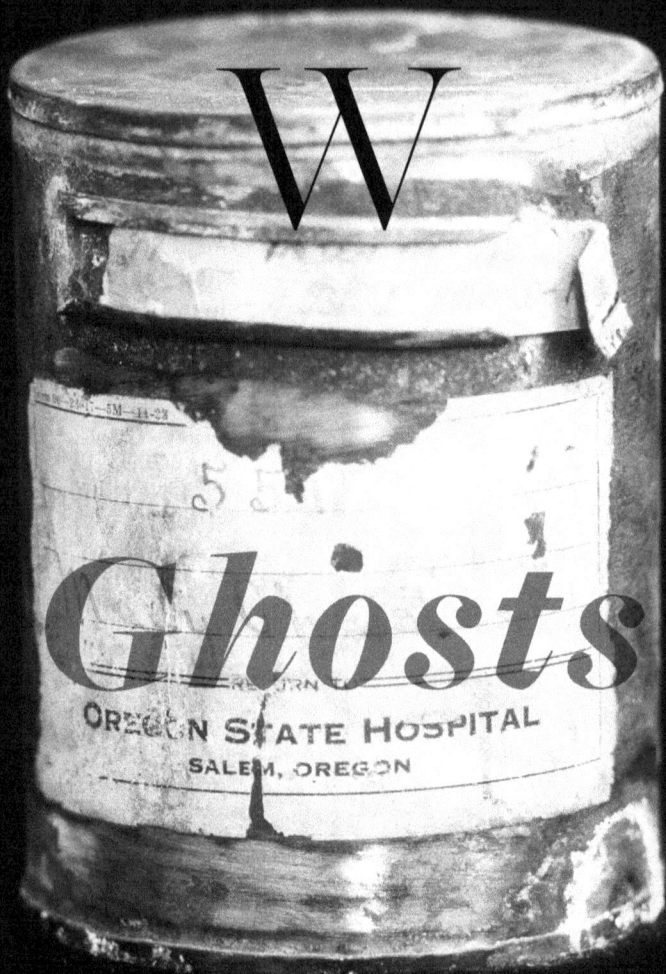

W

Ghosts

RETURN TO

OREGON STATE HOSPITAL

SALEM, OREGON

DAVID MAISEL / INSTITUTE

WITNESS XXVII.1 *Ghosts* on sale now at witnessmag.com
Submissions for non-themed online issues open Sept. 1 - Dec. 1

Beverly Rogers, Carol C. Harter
BLACK MOUNTAIN
I N S T I T U T E

A publication of Black Mountain Institute
at the University of Nevada, Las Vegas

Submit to Bear Review

Poetry / Flash Fiction
Micro Essays / Art

bearreview.com

A L M O S T   R A I N
SIMON PERCHIK

From earlier books:

"At Corinth, two temples stood next to one another: one to violence and one to necessity. Mr. Perchik's poems attend both temples, and are often terrifying compressions of the violence in simple daily acts." **Paul Blackburn**

"So much of what Perchik does include (but leaves at the heart level) is this important thing and I always hear it, as he knows, in what he does." **Charles Olson**

"Much like William Bronk or Jack Spicer, Perchik is a poet's poet…of deep, brooding poems that reflect and encompass an amazing spectrum of human experience…refracted through the eyes and mind of an exceptionally gifted poet." **Rain Taxi**

"This is certainly no derivative collection, but rather a unique meditation on the orogeny of a soul." **Boston Review**

"Perchik is the most widely published unknown poet in America ... who may well be our era's Emily Dickinson. **Library Journal**

"What is always clear is that this is a complex, lyrical vision of the commonplace. Even a meager narrative is hardly worth noticing, finally, in the midst of these exquisite imaginings. It is the constant struggle in this process which empowers his poetry and provides tension to his lyric." **Mid-American Review**

"...working close to the deeper sources of poetry, in modes reflecting individuality and technical determination, Mr. Perchik is the most original..." **Poetry**

"Let others jockey for position. Perchik's poems are obdurant and honest and will reach those who need them most." **James Tate**

"Simon Perchik's extraordinary lyric talent is one of the best kept secrets in contemporary American poetry. His surreal leaps orchestrate very personal material into archetypal configurations that approach transcendence." **Edward Butscher**

Mr. Perchik's poetry has been published in Partisan Review,
The Nation, Poetry and The New Yorker.
For more information on Simon Perchik, go to
www.simonperchik.com

River Otter Press
PO Box 211664   St. Paul, MN 55121
RiverOtterPress@gmail.com
Soft Cover $12.99 available on Amazon.com
Hard Cover $29.99 available at RiverOtterPress@gmail.com

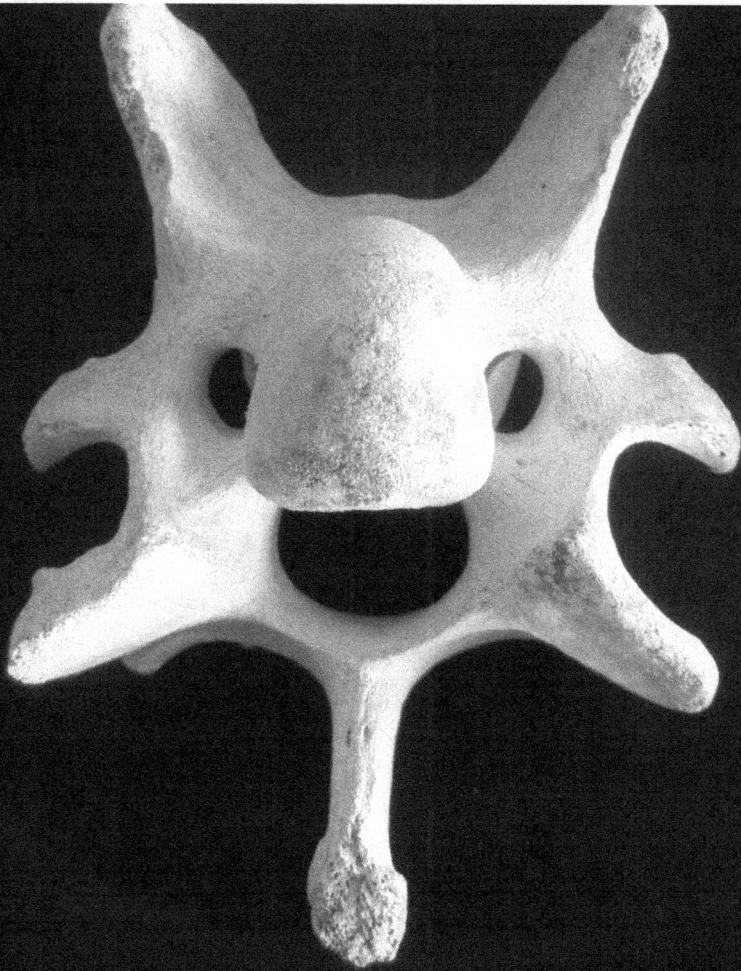

M o o by Paula C. Lowe

Rooted in rural earth…these are poems of extraordinary focus from "the neck of a kitten" to the "spit of a warlords' speech." --- Molly Best Tinsley, FUZE

Available at BigYesPress.com & Amazon.com

The Seattle Review
announces its inaugural
Chapbook Contest

Judged by Ben Lerner

1st Prize - receives $1,000 & 20 copies of the chapbook, which will be designed & printed by Paper Hammer

2 Finalists - each receive $100 & publication in *The Seattle Review*

From **May 1st to June 31st**, submit 20-30 pages of
poetry along with a reading fee. The $20 entry fee includes a one-year subscription to *The Seattle Review*. There is a $25 entry fee if you would also like to receive a copy of the winning chapbook. Online submissions only. Please visit www.seattlereview.org for more information.

You Are Here

Light drips down
from the capitol dome. Coffee
flows up through
veins, and all is not for
nothing, governor, nothing
is for naught when it's made
for the benefit of everyone and the self
walking certain streets at
an uncertain hour

Certain Streets at an
Uncertain Hour:
The Kansas Papers

poems by
Jeff Tigchelaar

coming Fall 2014

saltfront

arts and literary journal

We are searching for new ways to tell stories of what it means to be human amidst the monumental ecological transformations taking place on this planet.

Issue 2 available in May

reading period for
Issue 3 opens June 15

www.saltfront.org
saltfront@gmail.com

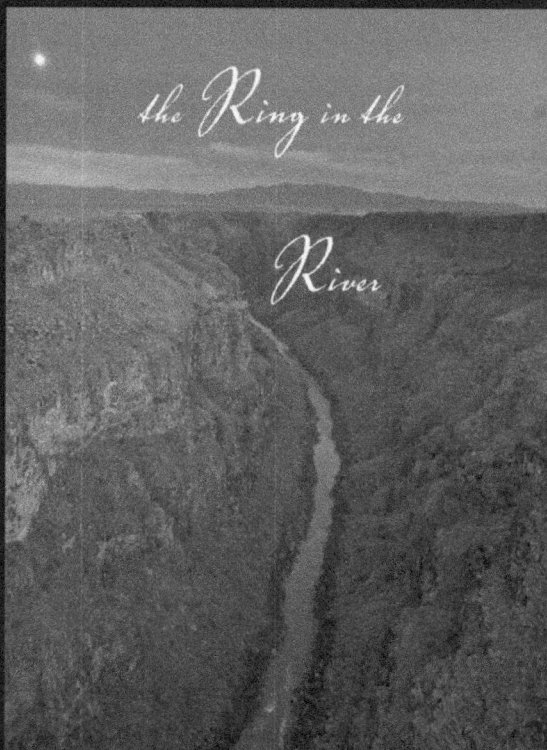

Losing

the Ring in the

River

MARGE SAISER

LOSING THE RING IN THE RIVER is a novel in poems, a story of three generations on the Great Plains, beginning with Clara and her abusive husband, Luke, working the land in the early 1900s, and continuing with Emma and Liz, who learn to take happiness where they can find it.

Available at Barnes & Nobel, Amazon, and at the University of New Mexico Press.

Too Much Breath

Available from the Main Street Rag Online Bookstore
www.MainStreetRag.com/bookstore/

or from the author
www.MartinBalgach.com

poems by

Martin Balgach

www.ingramcontent.com/pod-product-compliance
Lightning Source LLC
Chambersburg PA
CBHW070546030426
42337CB00016B/2366